To Tils & Ray, thank you for letting me be your weird, bug-loving big sister and for putting up with my silly ant-ics! Love you both lots xx
—M.K.

Published by Rocket Bird Books
an imprint of HarperCollins*Publishers* Limited,
1 London Bridge Street, London, SE1 9GF

www.rocketbirdbooks.co.uk

HarperCollins*Publishers*
Macken House, 39/40 Mayor Street Upper,
Dublin 1, D01 C9W8, Ireland

First published in Great Britain in 2025

Copyright © 2025 Moesha Kellaway

The moral rights of Moesha Kellaway to be identified as the author and illustrator of this work have been asserted in accordance with the Copyright, Designs and Patents Act, 1988.

Without limiting the exclusive rights of any author, contributor or the publisher of this publication, any unauthorised use of this publication to train generative artificial intelligence (AI) technologies is expressly prohibited. HarperCollins also exercise their rights under Article 4(3) of the Digital Single Market Directive 2019/790 and expressly reserve this publication from the text and data mining exception.

ISBN: 978-1-91539-520-7

10 9 8 7 6 5 4 3 2

All rights reserved.

A CIP record for this book is available from the British Library.

Printed in India

This book contains FSC™ certified paper and other controlled sources to ensure responsible forest management.

For more information visit: www.harpercollins.co.uk/green

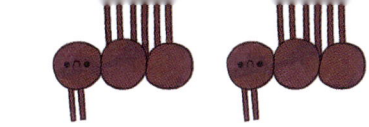

MOESHA KELLAWAY

ANT LIFE

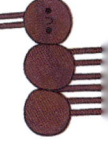

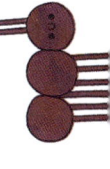

ROCKET BIRD BOOKS

I might be more of an outdoor ant. There are lots of sisters working hard out here. The first ones we meet are the anthill guards. Their job is to only let in ants from their own colony.

If you don't smell of our queen, you're not coming in.

What's your job?

Door.

DOOR HEAD ANTS

Some colonies' guards really use their heads... huge heads that block and hide the anthill entrance!

SCOUT SCHOOL

I'm nosy, so Chantal says I'd be an ace scout. I like finding food but I'm not sure about how they pass on news. Scout leader Santina says they swap smells, hit antennae and share food.

> Nope. Nope, nope, nope. I'm NOT going to eat another ant's vomit.

THE AMAZING ANT BODY

- ANTENNA (for smell, taste and touch)
- SECOND EYES (only see light and shadow)
- MOUTH
- MAIN EYES
- FEET
- LEGS
- STOMACHS

CLIMBER'S FEET

- INFLATABLE STICKY PAD
- HOOK

TWO TUMMIES

- SOCIAL STOMACH
- EATING STOMACH
- BUM

> When you find food, take a bite to store it in your social stomach. If you meet a fellow ant, vomit it up to share. Now two ants know about the new food!

SCENT CLASS

Ants have four times more smell-receptors than other insects. Smell is a kind of language for us.

FOOD THIS WAY
Once we ants find food, we need help getting it back to the colony, so we lay a scent-trail with our bums!

DANGER
We release this when the colony is under threat. It can smell like chocolate! Deliciously dangerous?

QUEEN
We're regularly coated in our queen's smell. When we meet another ant in the wild we can tell (smell!) if they are from our colony.

DEAD
This smell tells us to take away the body otherwise it could spread disease.

Dear Chantal,

Being a scout was not for me, but I loved the adventure. So...

I'M LEAVING TO SEE THE WORLD!

I want to meet foreign ants and find out about their work. I might even discover the perfect job for me. I promise to write lots of letters so you will know all about my travels.

Love,

Anita

WHERE DO ANTS LIVE?

- 0
- 1 – 19
- 20 – 139
- 140 – 10006

HOW MANY SPECIES OF ANT LIVE IN EACH AREA?

Dear Diary,

I feel nervous about setting off. The world is a dangerous place, especially with humans around. Luckily there are about 2.5 million ants for every human (yep, there's roughly 20 quadrillion of us).

My map shows where ants live – the darker the red, the more ant species!

ANT ARCHITECTS

Ever since the colony job fair I've known we ants are amazing builders. But the nests I've seen on my travels are on another level!

"An elephant's no match for us!"

↰ THORNY HOME

Small but mighty, acacia ants live inside the acacia tree thorns. In return for a home and nectar, they protect the tree from things that eat it, like elephants.

BUILDING BIG

Red wood ants like to cover their nest with a thatched roof made of leaves, twigs and pine needles. Their anthill can be 2 metres high!

THIS IS NUTS!

Think acacia ants are tiny? Meet the acorn ants who love squeezing into small spaces. A whole colony can live inside an acorn.

RED WOOD ANTS' THATCHED NEST TOWERING OVER A HUMAN

WEAVING TOGETHER

Weaver ants make their homes in the treetops by sticking leaves together. And where do they get their glue? Why, it's the sticky silk their larvae normally use to weave their cocoons!

"Being a tube of glue is a lot of pressure!"

CARVING OUT

Carpenter ants are exactly what you think — they tunnel into wood to make their nests inside old trees and stumps.

LIVING ROOM

Army ants are always moving from one place to another, so they are experts at making their nests from . . . themselves!

A LIVING ARMY-ANT TENT TO KEEP THE REST OF THE COLONY DRY

ULTIMATE COMBAT-ANT

Deep in the Cambodian jungle, General Formiga shows me the ultimate ant soldiers, each with a special power...

BULLET ANT

SIZE: 20-40MM

POWER: FIERY STING

HOME: CENTRAL & SOUTH AMERICA

ANT RATING: 🐜🐜🐜🐜🐜

The most painful sting in the insect world, the fiery agony lasts for 24 hours.

LEAFCUTTER ANT

SIZE: 16MM

POWER: GIANT BITE & CRYSTAL ARMOUR

HOME: SOUTH MEXICO TO BRAZIL

ANT RATING: 🐜🐜🐜🐜

A huge jaw gives a painful bite while thousands of crystals form hard armour.

It's not just weapons that make a great army. Being able to heal your comrades means you always have enough fighters.

Tell that to the exploding ant with the toxic goo.

JACK JUMPER

SIZE: 14MM

POWER: GIANT JUMP

HOME: AUSTRALIA

ANT RATING: 🐜🐜🐜🐜🐜

A very aggressive ant that can leap 76mm (5 times their length) in one jump.

EXPLODING ANT

SIZE: 4–8MM

POWER: TOXIC GOO

HOME: S.E. ASIA

ANT RATING: 🐜🐜🐜

These worker ants grab an enemy and explode, covering them with toxic goo.

RED WOOD ANT

SIZE: 4.5–9MM

POWER: ACID SPRAY

HOME: EUROPE & RUSSIA

ANT RATING: 🐜🐜🐜🐜

They don't have stingers, but spray acid at enemies from centimetres away.

MATABELE ANT

SIZE: 20MM

POWER: HEALING

HOME: AFRICA

ANT RATING: 🐜🐜🐜🐜🐜

These termite-hunters carry home their injured and nurse them.

MILKING

APHID MILKER

This job is sweet! Rub an aphid with your antenna and they poo out honeydew.

HERDING

Aphid farmer-ants take their herd to the juiciest part of the plant.

PROTECTING

"Buzz off Ladybird!"

And they fight off creatures that want to eat their aphid herd.

> ANITA, COME HOME AS SOON AS YOU CAN. I CAN'T TELL YOU WHY. LOVE, CHANTAL x

I could keep exploring forever, but Chantal needs me at the anthill.

BEST WORKER AWARDS

I don't believe it – Chantal's been sharing my letters in the colony newspaper. Everyone has been reading them, even the Queen! I'm getting an award for a job I didn't even know I was doing: roving reporter, now royal correspond-ant!

 # The Anthill Herald

REPORTER GETS GOLD!
ANITA NAMED ROYAL CORRESPOND-ANT

Worker Awards Night

Our own travel-reporter, Anita, has tonight been awarded a gold medal for being one of the year's best worker ants. Asked how she felt, Anita said:

"I didn't know this WAS a job! I just love travelling. It was my sister Chantal who shared my letters with the whole colony."

Anita was very happy that everyone had enjoyed her reports and she can't wait to get back out into the wide world of ants.

Anita got another surprise: HRH Queen Melisant has named her Royal Reporter. A great honour for any worker ant, especially the world's "laziest" one.

To read Anita's latest adventure and find out about her plans for the future, turn to page 5.